This Book is a Gift for

_____

From

_____

Date

_____

"This is a magnificent little book
about the marvel of Easter
for you to share with your little ones."

Abbot Luke Rigby, O.S.B.

Published by Liguori Publications
Liguori, Missouri 63057

To order, call 800-325-9521
Liguori.org

ISBN 978-0-7648-2353-4

Liguori Publications, a nonprofit corporation, is an apostolate of The Redemptorists.
To learn more about The Redemptorists, visit Redemptorists.com.

Printed in the United States of America

23 22 21 20 19 / 7 6 5 4 3

Typographic Design by Trese Gloriod

Easter Bunny's Amazing Day

Written by
Carol Benoist and
Cathy Gilmore

Illustrated by
Jonathan Sundy

Liguori

Hi!

I'm the Easter Bunny.

But I wasn't always
the Easter Bunny.

Can I tell you
my story?

Long ago,
when I was just a little
bunny, I lived with my
mama, my papa, and
my brothers and sisters . . .

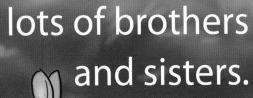

lots of brothers
and sisters.

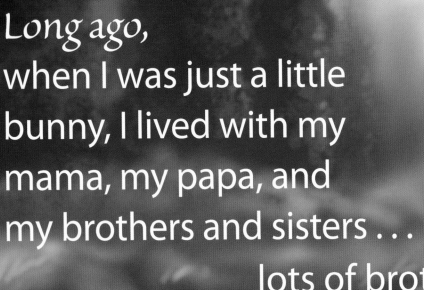

We lived in a really beautiful garden, and we had plenty of yummy grass to eat.

I had young animal
friends to play with too.

My best friend was a mouse.
He was really good at
hide and go seek.

I was just really good at . . .

hiding.

You see,
I had a problem.

I was afraid . . .

of nearly everything,
        nearly all the time.
I was afraid of the DARK.
I was afraid of THUNDER.
            LIGHTNING.
                SHADOWS.
                    CROWDS.

And especially,
HORSES.

One time,
I had to dart out from under
a horse's pounding hoof
when a group of riders
came galloping through
the garden.

I was so scared ... I shivered,
and I could hardly eat for a week.

The only thing scarier
than *horses*
was the dark and gloomy *CAVE*
at the corner of the garden.

I could never go in it.

One time, everything I was afraid of happened on the same day.

It started with *riders on horses*
yelling at a *crowd* of people
going past the garden.

Later on, it grew Dark...
in the middle of the day!

Then there was a tremendous *Storm*
with **Thunder**
and **Lightning**.

Even the ground *shook* under me.

I cowered in the corner

for a long

...long time.

Later
the storm
ended, and a
group of people
came into the
cave holding
torches.

They brought a man wrapped
in white cloths and laid him
on a flat piece of rock.

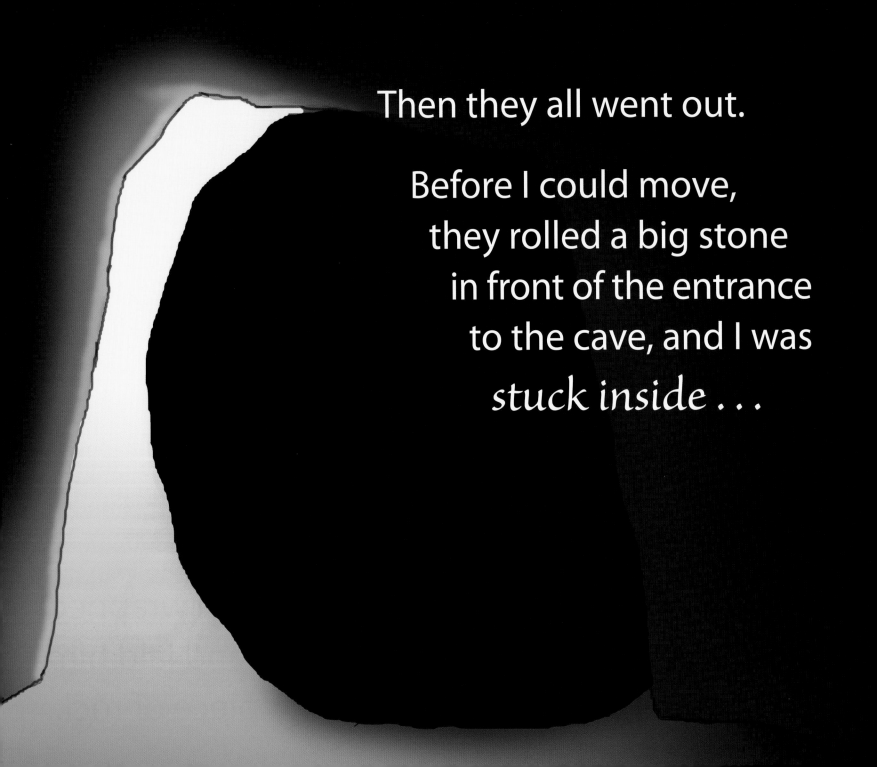

Then they all went out.

Before I could move,
they rolled a big stone
in front of the entrance
to the cave, and I was

stuck inside . . .

in the dark!

I was in there for three days
with the man wrapped in white cloth.

There was something about him.

At least I wasn't alone.

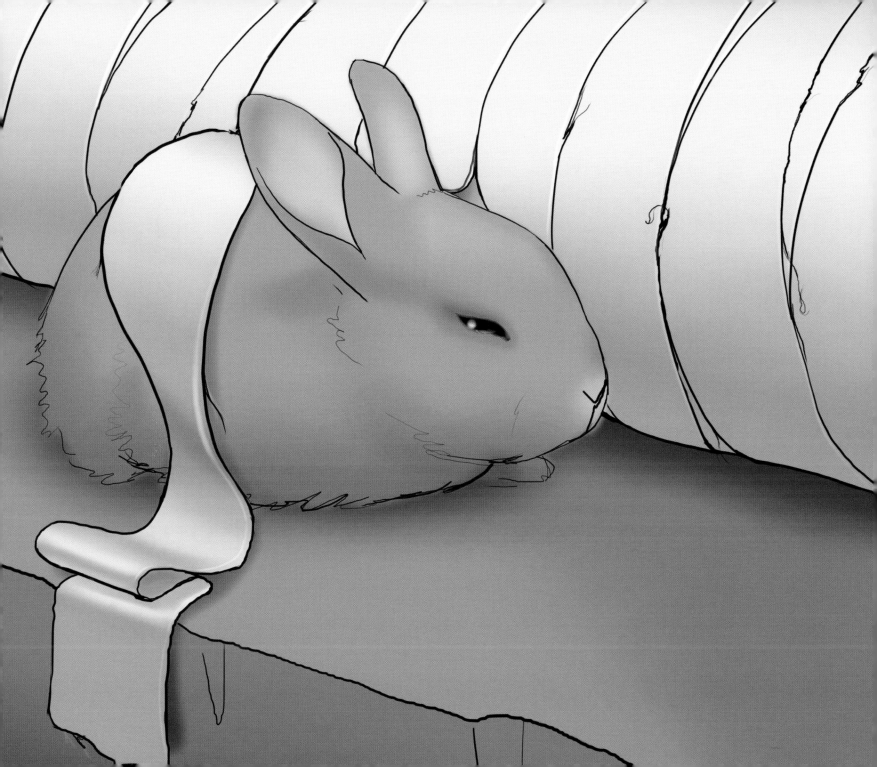

Then, the most *amazing* thing happened.

The cave filled with a light so bright I could barely see.

The man got up.

The light was coming from him.

He glowed.

There was a sound
of air SWOOSshhing into the cave
like the room was taking
a deep breath of the freshest air
in the whole world.

As the air whooshed back out,
the stone rolled away
and the cave was open again!

Light streamed in and out.

I inched forward a little bit.
The man saw me.

I wanted to run.

He stooped down
and held out his hand
and smiled at me.

When I saw his eyes,
I didn't want to run away
anymore.

With my front paws,
I stepped up onto
his warm fingers
and sniffed.

His touch made me feel warm inside.

He scooped me up,
held me close to his heart,
and took me outside.

He stroked my fur
with gentle hands
and said,

"Don't be afraid, Little Bunny.
I am with you."

Hearing His voice . . .

I knew I'd never be afraid again.

The special day when the man who glowed came out of the dark is called *Easter*.

They call me the
Easter Bunny
because that was
the *amazing* day
He took all
my fears away.

Thank You, Jesus, for Easter, and for everything.